Please return / renew this item by the last day shown

OXFORDSHIRE
COUNTY COUNCIL
LEARNING & CULTURE
www.oxfordshire.gov.uk

IMAGES OF ENGLAND

THE STORY OF
THE HENLEY COLLEGE

GEMMA ALLEN

TEMPUS

Frontispiece: Henley Grammar School was housed at Rotherfield Court from 1928 and the buildings were also used by its successor, King James's College. Rotherfield is now one of the sites used by The Henley College.

First published 2004

Tempus Publishing Limited
The Mill, Brimscombe Port,
Stroud, Gloucestershire, GL5 2QG
www.tempus-publishing.com

British Library Cataloguing in Publication Data.
A catalogue record for this book is available from the British Library.

ISBN 0 7524 3246 X

Typesetting and origination by Tempus Publishing Limited.
Printed in Great Britain.

Contents

Acknowledgements

The idea for this book was formed during history lessons in my first year at The Henley College. Those lessons always took place in the old attics at Rotherfield. The attics were wonderfully atmospheric little rooms and, together with the rest of the building, they inspired me to learn more about the history of the College. I must therefore firstly thank The Henley College for allowing me to satisfy that curiosity, so fortunately awakened a few years before the 400th anniversary of the Grammar School's foundation.

Many people and organisations, both in Henley-on-Thames and beyond, have proved integral to the completion of this research. I am indebted to the following for providing both information and images for the publication: Mr Aldridge, Mrs Cheriton, Kenneth Clarke, Diane Cook, Frank Cordrey, Ann Cottingham, Hilary Fisher, Linda Hall, John Howard, Dr John Pither, Vic Reeves, Margaret Shaida, The Henley Educational Charity, Richard Reed and Mary Schriven of the *Henley Standard*, Mark Geleta and Liz Walker of IJP Building Conservation Ltd, the librarians at the Local Studies Centre in Henley Library, Jane Bowen, Ditte Hviid and Emily Leach of the River and Rowing Museum.

I must also thank the Tate Gallery for permission to reproduce Silberecht's *Landscape with Rainbow, Henley-on-Thames* on page 15; the National Portrait Gallery for the image of Archbishop Laud on page 18; the Bodleian Library for permission to reproduce Buckler's paintings on pages 15, 18 and 21; the *Henley Standard* for the image on page 28. The staff of the Oxfordshire Photographic Archive, particularly Nuala LaVertu and Dr Malcolm Grey, have been of immense help during my research, as have the staff of the Oxfordshire Record Office. Images from their collections appear throughout the work.

I owe a debt of gratitude to many Old Henleiensians, both staff and pupils, without whom this publication could not have been completed. My sincere thanks go to the following: Revd and Mrs Attrill, Tony Austin, Anne Bonwit, Alan Bowyer, Philip Brown, Geoff Butler, Brian Collins, Rhoda Cope, Gill Davies, Keith and Marjorie Dawson, George Francis, Jeremy Goldwyn, David and Norah Henschel, Richard Hewitt, John Hocking, Tony Hobbs, Audrey Rooks, Beryl Swan, Monica Tomalin, Chris Walker, Sandra Wickens, Noel Younger.

Present staff of The Henley College have also given me considerable help with the project and I would like to thank David Ansell, Lynnette Beanland, Maree Dudding, Ellen MacHale and the Henley College Librarians, Andy Pegg, Nic Saunders, Mark Turauskis, Nigel Watts and my father, Peter Allen.

Any acknowledgements would not be complete without expressing my thanks to my whole family and to Edward Arnold for living with this research for many months. The multiplicity of institutions that together form the history of The Henley College always indicated that this would not be a straightforward project, yet simultaneously it has never been a dull one. In the words of an early HGS School hymn, 'Vivat Semper Schola Nostra, Henleiensis Gloria' – whatever the name of the school.

Gemma Allen, 2004

Introduction

The story of The Henley College begins over four centuries ago. Its history far precedes the College's recent foundation in 1987 with the union of King James's College and the South Oxfordshire Technical College. Through these institutions The Henley College has a past which includes Henley's nineteenth-century 'Technical School of Science and Art' and stretches back to the foundation of Henley Grammar School in 1604.

The history of the College therefore begins with the foundation of the Free Grammar School at the beginning of the seventeenth century. Yet even before the Reformation, there are hints of a Grammar School within medieval Henley. The Bridgemen's accounts of 1420 mention that Robert Symon was 'scholemayster', teaching in the Chantry House. Bishop Longland of Lincoln, a native and benefactor of Henley, seems to have refounded or enlarged this school; Lily's Grammar was dedicated to him in 1532 with the comment 'for the use of Henley School'. The Chantry House, however, passed into private ownership when the Reformation initiated the abolition of religious endowments. Losing its buildings, the school seems to have closed. Twenty-five years passed before the Corporation of Henley began to think again about establishing another grammar school in the town. They bought back the Chantry House in 1578 and now had a building in which they might hold the School once again, yet they lacked the endowments to fund it. It took another twenty-four years until they received the first money for refounding the Grammar School.

In November 1602, Augustus Knapp left the Corporation of Henley £200 in his will, stipulating that within two years of his death they should 'found and appoint one free grammar school for the instruction of youthful people'. The money was to be invested in land with a yearly income of £20, which was to be used to pay a schoolmaster. Within the two years, the people of Henley successfully petitioned the new King for a Charter. The story of The Henley College thus truly begins in 1604, with the foundation of the Free Grammar School of King James I 'for the education, institution and instruction of children and youth in grammar and other good learning to endure for ever in time to come'.

While the Free Grammar School was operating on the upper floor of the Chantry House, another school was founded in Henley, housed on the lower floor of the same building. Dame Elizabeth Periam established and endowed her Charity School in 1609 'for the education in writing, reading, and casting accounts (but not for grammar learning), clothing, and apprenticing twenty poor boys of the said town'.

Both schools were provided with land and properties locally for their maintenance, but the Grammar School's endowments began to prove increasingly inadequate. The dwindling value of its stipends meant that the Grammar School was often reliant on unsuitable masters. Henry Munday, elected in 1653, proved a deficient master, while leading the school for over a quarter of a century. He used the post as an opportunity to pursue his own interest in physics and wrote a book, published in 1680, entitled *De Aere Vitali, de Esculentis, de Potulentis – Air and Life, Food and Drink*. In his work, Munday argues that coffee, for those of a full bodily habit, is often valuable, but does not suit the bilious or melancholic. Devoting his time to private study, Munday neglected the school and was about to be dismissed from his post when he died in a fall from his horse in 1682. Almost a century later another unsatisfactory candidate, Mr Neale, acted as master before he too was removed. A parent, Mr Rackstraw, testified that Mr Neale did not correct his son's exercises but threw them on the table. Neale was accused of sometimes shutting the school for two or three weeks at a time, although he continued to take the fees. It was also recorded that the scandalous Mr Neale had been heard to say that he did not care whether he had any pupils or not.

By the late eighteenth century, the Grammar School had neither the curriculum, as the master was not obliged to teach English, nor even the endowments to meet the approval of the people of Henley. Dame Periam's school could have supplied a more suitable education and had the resources to do so, for her endowments were steadily increasing in value. Yet her archaic statutes ordered that no more than twenty scholars could be educated in her school. The two Stuart institutions were becoming obsolete and the governors of the schools decided that they should join them into one institution. Parliament was petitioned and in 1778 passed an Act amalgamating the two schools.

They were henceforth to be known as the 'United Charity Schools of Henley-on-Thames', with an Upper School of twenty-five boys supplied from a Lower School of sixty boys. As the Chantry House was now proving cramped, the schools moved to premises on the south side of Hart Street. Over time, however, the two schools proved anything but united. The Charity Commissioners of 1819 found that for many years the two schools had not even been held in the same house and there were no attempts made to move boys on from the Lower to Upper Schools. In 1841, the schools moved to the former site of the Bell Inn at Northfield End, yet the two institutions still remained essentially separate until 1892. That year the Charity Commissioners drew up a new scheme for the United Charity Schools. The two foundations would from then on be joined into one school – a day and boarding school for boys between eight and sixteen. There were still to be ten Periam scholars drawn from the locality and they would be exempt from tuition fees. Under the Commission's scheme, this new school would be called Henley Grammar School.

In the years leading up to the First World War, Henley Grammar School occupied an increasingly difficult financial position. The 1902 Balfour Act had launched a new system of secondary education for all. The County Councils were now the local authorities of education and small endowed grammar schools, such as the Henley school, faced a struggle for financial survival. From 1904, Henley Grammar School received a small grant from the County Council in addition to its dwindling endowments. Yet this was insufficient to improve the buildings, which was necessary before the school could apply for the County Council grant it so desperately needed. Mr Valpy's strong leadership did much to improve the fortunes of HGS; when he was appointed headmaster in 1903, there were only forty boys at the school, yet by 1909 it had increased to sixty boys. For ten years the governors worked on the premises at Northfield End, turning dormitories into classrooms and creating new laboratories. By 1918 they had improved the school sufficiently to obtain a County Council grant, which now equalled the income from the endowments. A condition of the grant was that a quarter of the school had to comprise of ex-elementary school students. After the First World War, Henley Grammar School therefore consisted of fee-paying pupils, ten Periam scholars and the County Scholars.

Another great year of change for Henley Grammar School came in 1928. Yielding to pressure to become a County Council School, Henley Grammar School was moved to Rotherfield Court. It was fitted out as a modern secondary school to accommodate the boys and, for the first time, an equal number of girls. Until the Education Act of 1944, the school remained fee-paying. When the Grammar School was taken over by the County Council, a Foundation Trust was formed to distribute the income from the school's endowments; the money was then used to provide scholarships to the Grammar School. After the 1944 Act abolished fee-paying in County-run schools, the 11+ was adopted as a means of selection. Following the calls for secondary reorganisation along comprehensive lines, HGS then adopted the compromise of selection at 13+ in 1966, which involved children being selected from a 'federation' of three local secondary schools – Gillotts, Langtree and Chiltern Edge. Six years later, in the face of serious local misgivings, public notice was given that education in south Oxfordshire would become comprehensive. From 1974, Henley Grammar School consequently ceased admitting younger pupils, who were accommodated in the three local 11–16 schools. Two years later, Henley Grammar School was replaced by King James's Sixth Form College.

The character of King James's College was firmly established by David Henschel, its first principal, who had also been headmaster of the Grammar School since 1966. He secured permission from the Crown to name the College after its original founder, King James I, and also ensured that traditions were continued in this new establishment.

Just along the road from King James's College was the South Oxfordshire Technical College. A close relationship was maintained between the institutions, which had been initiated with the formation of the Centre for Advanced Studies in 1967, then comprising of Henley Grammar School and the Technical College. Yet like its close neighbour, the Technical College also had a long history, which stretched back to its foundation in 1873 in Hart Street as the 'Technical School of Science and Art'. By the end of the nineteenth century, the Institute was housed in Duke Street, on the floor above the Free Reading Room. After a few years based on the Reading Road from 1953, the Institute moved to the former site of the National School on Gravel Hill. It officially opened on that site as a full-time institution in 1962, renamed the 'South Oxfordshire Technical College'.

King James's and the Technical College together developed a common timetable which allowed students to study in both institutions. Over a hundred students took this opportunity to combine academic subjects with vocational ones. By the 1980s, however, King James's remained the only Sixth Form College in the area and calls for a merger started to gather momentum. Meetings were held in 1984 to debate the principle of a tertiary college and finally in January 1985 the governors of both King James's College and the Technical College gave their approval to a single tertiary college 'combining the best traditions of the two existing colleges'.

The Henley College, Oxfordshire's first tertiary college, was therefore established in 1987. The College was, and continues to be, a popular focus in the town, as it offers an unparalleled range of courses as well as the opportunity for students to develop as independent people within a supportive atmosphere.

Yet the modern College still has many links with its past. The Periam Lectures held every year honour the seventeenth-century founder by inviting highly influential speakers to the College. The Foundation Trust, formed when the Grammar School came under County Council control, still oversees the ancient endowments as the Henley Educational Charity, with a charitable interest in all the schools in Henley. Yet perhaps the strongest link with the past is the quality of education provided at The Henley College, which remains outstanding and surely fulfils the wishes of King James I, who in 1604 founded an institution to provide 'good learning to endure for ever in time to come'.

HENLEY GRAMMAR SCHOOL

The School Hymn

LORD! keep our School, for-
ever in Thy hand
   Stainless and bright;
True lore professing, ever let
it stand
   A beacon light:
So, when we launch away on
life's rough sea,
May we look back, and know
we look to Thee.

LORD! keep our School; our
lives are in Thy hand;
   Our moments seem
In Thy turned hour-glass,
grains of running sand,
   Ours to redeem;
Transmuted store with golden
action fraught,
Touched by her spirit, to
Thy treasury brought.

LORD! keep our School, our
times are in Thy hand,
   Past, and to be;
We learn a part; by Thee the
whole is planned;
   Teach us to see
Our youth to age can only
pass aright,
If led by Thee, in Whom all
times unite.

LORD! keep our School, a
jewel to Thy hand,
   Bright with Thy gleam,
Till that dark angel tells o'er
sea and land
   Time was dream;
Clear through our waking
may its memory shine
And make us blest to know
our School was Thine.

Michael Mason.

The HGS Hymn, written by Michael Mason, was used after the school's move to Rotherfield Court in 1928. Before then, when HGS was at Northfield End, it seems that another hymn was sung, yet it expressed a similar pride in the Grammar School. The chorus was '*Vivat Semper Schola Nostra/Henleiensis Gloria*' – 'May the Glory of our Henley School Forever Flourish'.

one

'Good learning to
endure for ever in
time to come'
1604–1778

The Free Grammar School of King James I and Dame Periam's Charity School

Augustus Knapp left £200 in his will of 1602, specifying that within two years of his death the people of Henley should 'found and appoint one free grammar school for the instruction of youthful people'. The Free Grammar School was thus founded by James I in 1604 'for the education, institution and instruction of children and youth in grammar and other good learning to endure for ever in time to come'. The school was housed on the upper floor of the Chantry House, a building lying adjacent to St Mary's Church in Henley. Running in parallel with the Free Grammar School was Dame Elizabeth Periam's Charity School. She founded her Charity School in 1609 and it was held below the Grammar School, on the lower floor of the Chantry House. This may have led to them becoming known as the Upper and Lower Grammar Schools, although they were two entirely separate institutions at this stage of their history; the aim of Dame Periam's school was to prepare twenty poor boys of the town for an apprenticeship, so her pupils were not educated in grammar. By the end of the eighteenth century it was clear that the statutes, which prescribed the type of education provided at each of the schools, were becoming obsolete. The people of Henley were thus inspired to try and unite the two schools into one institution.

An illustration of James I from the Grammar School's Royal Charter. The Charter stated that prayers were to be said twice a day at the school, in which the scholars were to give hearty thanks and praise unto God for the King's Majesty, James I, the sole and only founder of the said school. Small mention is made of Augustus Knapp, who provided the first £200 to establish the school; he is referred to only as its first and especial benefactor.

The exterior of the Chantry House, where the Grammar School was housed on the first floor. Boys had to attend from 6 a.m. in the summer, 7 a.m. in the winter, and they worked until 11 a.m. After they returned to school at 1 p.m., lessons then continued until 5 p.m.

The interior of the upper floor of the Chantry House. The seventeenth-century school would not have filled the room with much equipment. The school owned four blackboards at 2s 6d, along with benches, long forms and bellows. The Charter with its great seal, along with the school statutes, was kept in a specially made box. Important events, such as the restoration of Charles II in 1660, were commemorated by the setting up of the Royal Arms in the school.

The seal of the Free Grammar School of King James I. Although the seal describes the school as 'free', boys had to pay 12d to the master, and 6d to the Usher, upon first joining the school and 4d quarterly thereafter. The school was thus for the sons of the lower orders in Henley who had received enough preparatory learning to undertake a classical education and whose families could afford the entrance fees.

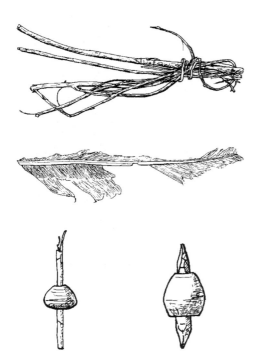

During restoration of the upper floor of the Chantry House in 2004, a master's switch, fragments of quill pens and some spinning tops were found under the floorboards; the archaeologist's illustrations are shown to the left. The spinning tops suggest that some of the Grammar School's scholars may have flouted the school statutes, which stated that 'No scholar shall play within the School at any Game at all'. The statutes of 1612 go on to add that 'neither shall he elsewhere out of the School play at any unlawful or hurtful Game as Football play, Dice or Cards, Tables or Trunks, neither shall they play at any Games for Money, or for any thing of value, neither shall they presume or adventure to swim or wash themselves in the River without leave obtained of their master'.

William Gravett, a solicitor of Lyon's Inn in London, left in his will of 1664 certain lands in Henley, to be used to provide a house for the schoolmaster of the Grammar School. Gravett reasoned that the master 'having a more competent maintenance and some fit house to dwell in, might, with more cheerful industry and alacrity teach and instruct'.

The Chantry House, where the school was housed, had a storehouse and granaries reaching down to the river. The school claimed wharfage dues from any barges docking along this stretch of river, as shown in the above detail from Jan Siberecht's *Landscape with Rainbow, Henley-on-Thames* (*c*. 1690). The charge in 1670 was 4d a load and wharfage dues were being claimed by the school from those docking anywhere from the Red Lion down to the corner of New Street. The school lost a dispute over wharfage dues with the Lord of the Manor in 1730 and from then on could only collect tolls from the wharf directly in front of the Chantry House.

The General Register of the Free Grammar School from 1604 to 1777 still exists and contains the school's library lists for 1627 and 1658, revealing that thirty-one and twenty-nine books were respectively held. The book shown to the right, recently discovered during restoration to the Chantry House, is included in these library lists. Latin texts make up half the library, but there are also two mathematical books, one Greek work and a Latin Bible. The rest are dictionaries and grammars. The books reflect the classical education offered by the school: Latin and a little arithmetic, geometry and Greek.

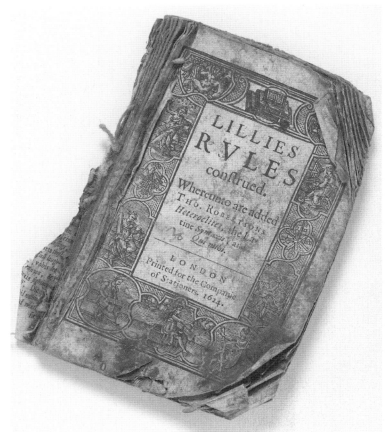

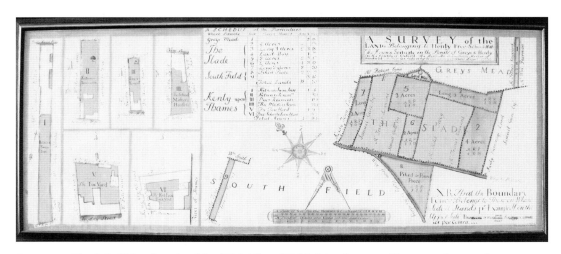

A survey of lands held by the school in 1726. The £200 left by Augustus Knapp to finance the school had been invested in land and property in Henley, including three tenements in what was then called Gravelly Hill (now Gravel Hill). The school also held land donated by James I in 1604, then amounting to the value of £11 17s 4d, as well as land left by William Gravett in 1664.

MEMORIAE SACRVM DIGNISSIMAE FEMINAE DOMINAE ELIZAE
PERIAM VIDVAE QVONDAM VXORIS PRIMO ROBBERTI
DOYLEY DENVO HENRICI NEVILE VLTIMO GVLIELMI
PERIAM MILITVM QVAE IN HOC OPPIDO SCHOLAM FVND
AVIT EDVCANDIS PAVPERVM FILIIS VICINTI ET BAILIOLEN
COLLE CIVM IN INCLYTA ACADEMIA OXON VNIVS
SOCII ET DVORVM SCHOLARVM ACCESSIONE
DOTAVIT. OBIIT AVTEM ANNO DOMINI MILLESIMO
SESCENTESIMO VICESIMO PRIMO MAII TERTIO.

Dame Periam founded her school in 1609 'for the education in writing, reading, and casting accounts (but not for grammar learning), clothing, and apprenticing twenty poor boys of the said town'. She endowed the school with land around Henley and from that income she decreed for her pupils that 'there shall be bestowed yearly at Easter £12 in broad cloath to make them dublets and breeches and £3 for canvass to line the same. Each of them shall have one paire of stockings price sh.13, one paire of shoes price sh.2, cloth for 2 shirts and 2 bands, and the same to cost in the whole £3.10., and 10 sh. yearly to be allowed for the making of them'. The alabaster monument commemorating Dame Periam in St Mary's Church, Henley, shown above, was defaced during the Civil War. It was repaired in 1711 at the charge of Richard Jennings, Master Carpenter under Sir Christopher Wren of St Paul's Cathedral, who had received his education at Dame Periam's school by her charity.

Dame Periam's school paid a fee of 4s a year for use of the lower floor of the Chantry House. The number of scholars educated at the school was, by Dame Periam's orders, not to exceed twenty, with boys entering the school at nine or ten years old and staying until sixteen, if not apprenticed before.

Dame Periam's interest in education was due to the influence of William Laud, Archbishop of Canterbury from 1633 to 1645. Her commitment to educational provision was further shown by her endowment of Balliol College, Oxford with land in Hambleden and Princes Risborough for the creation of a Fellowship and two Scholarships, although no preference was to be shown to Henley scholars.

two
'Henleiensis Gloria'
1778-1928

From the United Charity Schools to Henley Grammar

The Free Grammar School and Dame Periam's Charity School were united by an Act of Parliament in 1778. The United Charity Schools, as they were collectively named, were to consist of an Upper and a Lower School. The Upper School, consisting of twenty-five boys, was to be supplied from the Lower School of sixty boys. There were to be twenty Blue Coat scholars whose fees would be paid from Lady Periam's charity, while the remainder were to pay an admission fee of 1s 6d, with a payment of 6d a quarter. The Chantry House now proved too small to house the United Charity Schools and they were moved to premises on the south side of Hart Street. Yet by 1826, *The Henley Guide* noted that 'a separate school and master is kept for each' and by this time the schools were only united in name. It took until 1892 for the schools to be finally joined as one by the Victorian Charity Commissioners. The schools then became known as Henley Grammar School. From the mid-nineteenth century '*Henleiensis Gloria*', the glorious Henley school named in an early HGS hymn, was housed on the site of the old Bell Inn in Northfield End, where it remained until 1928.

ANNO DECIMO OCTAVO

Georgii III. Regis.

C A P. XLI.

An Act for uniting the Free Grammar School of *James* King of *England*, within the Town of *Henley upon Thames*, in the County of *Oxford*, with the Charity School founded in the same Town by Dame *Elizabeth Periam* Widow; and for the better Regulation and Management of the said Endowments.

WHEREAS his Majesty King James the First, by his Letters Patent under the Great Seal of England, bearing Date on or about the Seventeenth Day of December, in the Second Year of his Reign of England, France, and Ireland, and the Thirty-eighth of Scotland, upon the humble Petition of the Inhabitants of the Town of Henley upon Thames, in the County of Oxford, did found a Grammar School in the said Town, for the Education, Institution, and Instruction of Youth in Grammar and other good Learning, endowing the same with certain Obiits,

9 E 2   Annual

According to the Act of Parliament of 1778, no boy could be elected to go from the Lower School into the Upper School until he could read competently, write in joined-up and cast a sum in pounds, shillings and pence. The Act also stated that twenty boys were still to be clothed annually according to Dame Periam's direction.

The old schoolrooms in the Chantry House were proving an inadequate home for the schools by 1792 and they were let to Barrett March of the Red Lion Hotel for £60 a year. The students moved across the road to premises on the south side of Hart Street. The School House was then a long brick and flint structure at the rear of Speaker's House and the above painting shows the north-west approach to the school.

Revd Scobell, master of the Upper School from 1803 to 1817, requested the use of the Lower School rooms in 1805, after the inhabitants of Henley raised objections over the amount of contact between boys of the two schools. Mr Chapman, master of the Lower School, then moved his boys into a room in his own house. The School House in Hart Street was thus left for the Upper School and master's residence.

The schools were granted a lease on the previous site of the Bell Inn at Northfield End in 1841. The Inn's business had suffered after the stage-coach traffic through Henley declined with the building of the Great Western Railway. Both the Upper and Lower School moved to these new premises, although the divisions between them were maintained. A sales catalogue of 1853 records the 'Lot' held by the trustees of the schools: 'Nine bedrooms and two small rooms adjoining. Entrance halls, two sitting rooms, dining room, kitchen, back ditto, two dressing rooms, school room and butler's pantry. Closet, housekeeper's room, knifehouse, cellar and playground and ornamental ground in front'.

Revd Godby became master in 1844 and the inhabitants of Henley praised his twenty-six year reign as being characterised by 'indefatigable exertions' and 'judicious firmness'. Godby's private connections attracted over fifty boarders to the school, who lived in a adjoining house rented by the master. The number of scholars increased so much during his headmastership that the Lower School had to move back to the old premises in Hart Street in 1846.

Mr G.W. Reeves started at the Upper Grammar School only two years after this etching was made in 1875. 'I had to part with my first and only chum as he was going to the Lower Grammar School', wrote Reeves of his first day. 'Therefore we solemnly shook hands, and said "Goodbye", until the time arrived that we had left school and could do as we liked, as at that period the feud between the two schools was very bitter, and if one was seen talking to any of our enemies he was immediately sent to Coventry for a long time... On half-holidays we had to take a pal when going for a walk, or bird-nesting, otherwise we might be caught napping by the opposition and get a smart tanning in exchange for his stone-throwing a week before.'

A previously unpublished photograph of the whole Upper Grammar School in 1879, consisting of two masters and twenty-three boys. Mr G.W. Reeves is the first boy on the left in the back row. The master at that time was a Revd Faulkner, shown in the photograph, who was assisted by his brother. Mr Reeves wrote that 'Both were clergymen and one with a very long beard, which caused us much amusement at different times.'

Right: In 1892, the two schools were joined to form Henley Grammar School and at this time some of the senior boys at the Grammar School had the special privilege of being able to wear bowler hats decorated with black and red ribbons. The origin of this tradition is uncertain, but it has been suggested that it might be a reference to the Alma Mater of one of the masters.

Below: The school had a small playground and possessed a four-oar boat, even entering crews in Henley Regatta in 1864 and 1865. A paddock of four-acres adjoining the school, Dry Leas, was leased yearly and was used by the boys for cricket and football, although the owner, who was one of the trustees, made a road across the middle, which proved a bitter grievance to the boys at this time.

Right: Mr Valpy was headmaster of Henley Grammar School from 1903 to 1931. Valpy was affectionately known as 'Old Jack' by the many boys he taught. One Old Boy, G.J. Nash, argued he was characterised by a 'manly godliness', manifested not just in the Bible readings he enforced on his boys, but also in 'his keenness that we should learn how to box so that... we should be able to uphold the right or chastise the "bounder" should he cross our path'.

Below: This photograph of the big schoolroom was taken during the first term of Mr Valpy's headmastership in 1903. Assembly was held in the room, and during teaching hours it was divided by red plush curtains into three form rooms. Heating was by stoves, seen in the left foreground, and gas pendants provided the lighting.

Above: The approach to the Grammar School, photographed around 1905. The curriculum at this time was narrow. The greater part of the boys' time was spent studying Latin and Mathematics. English Literature was hardly studied at all and Science consisted of lectures on the chemistry of air and water to two forms at once. Yet by 1909, the school under Mr Valpy had grown to over sixty and had three assistant masters overseeing four forms.

Right: A.F. Bracher, an old Henleiensian, wrote in 1924 of the 'glory' of the elm tree that grew outside the school, which 'threw out its wide arms as if rejoicing in its strength'. The tree was traditionally known as 'Prince Rupert's Elm', after Charles I's nephew. In 1642, during the Civil War, this flamboyant cavalry leader rode into Henley down the Fairmile, surprising the town into falling without a shot being fired. Rupert was said to have hung a parliamentary spy from the elm, which overshadowed the school for its whole duration at Northfield End.

An extremely rare early photograph of the entire Grammar School in 1911. The headmaster, Mr Valpy, is seen in the centre and a later mayor of Henley, A.R. Hobbs, is one of the boys. A few years later, in 1919, a system of houses was introduced in the school. One was named Valpy after the headmaster and the other Periam, in honour of the school's ancient benefactor.

Another house was added to the school organisation in 1922, Hambleden, after the then Chairman of the Governors, Lord Hambleden. Hambleden house consisted of those who lived north of a line running from Grey's Road down to Friday Street; those to the south of the line went into Valpy. All Periam Scholars, County Scholars and Free Places went into Periam house. Increasing the number of houses was intended to induce a friendly rivalry in work and games which would lead to an 'espirit de house' and that in turn, recorded the school magazine, *The Periam*, would induce a better 'espirit de school'.

Troops outside the school just before the First World War. This was a time of great change for the Grammar School. There was increasing pressure for the school to become co-educational and the school endowments were proving dwindling and insufficient. After a County Council grant was awarded in 1918, the school was comprised of fee-paying pupils, ten Periam scholars, while the rest were County Scholars.

An advert for Henley Grammar School placed in the *Henley and South Oxfordshire Standard* of January 1928, during the school's final months at Northfield End. Many of the boys at the Grammar School then had a long school day, for those who lived in Henley had to return in the evening to do prep. There were about 109 boys at HGS by the end of its time in Northfield End.

Scholastic.

ROYAL GRAMMAR SCHOOL,
HENLEY-ON-THAMES,
CHARTER 1604.

The object of the School is to provide, at a moderate cost, a Mathematical, Classical, Scientific and General Education of a high order,

Boarding Fees - 40 gns. per annum.
Tuition Fees - 12 gns. per annum.

The School is a centre for Cambridge Local Examinations. The Headmaster is assisted by a competent staff of Masters. For a list of successes during the past year, and for all particulars apply to the Head Master, J. H. J. VALPY, M.A., or to the Clerk, 2, West Street, Henley.

Next Term, Thursday, January 19th, 1928.

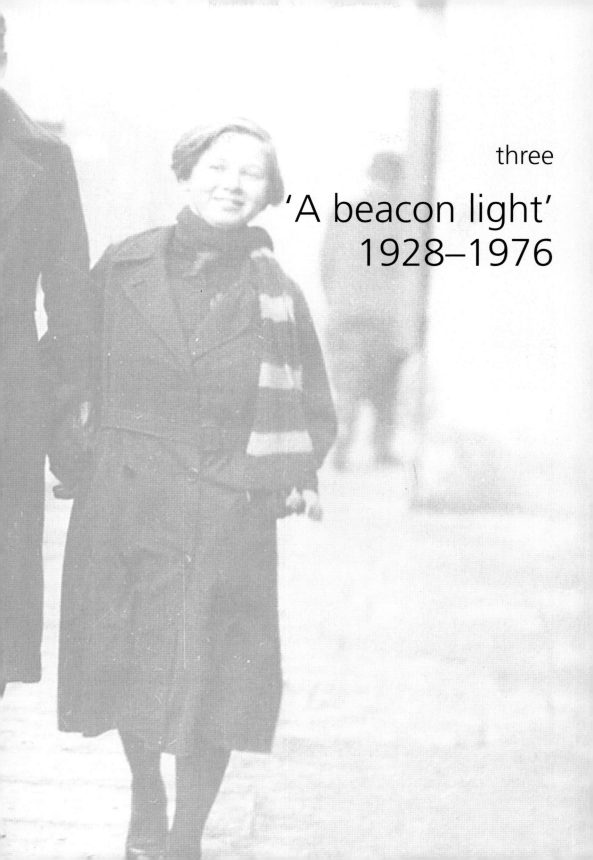

three

'A beacon light'
1928–1976

Henley Grammar School at Rotherfield

Henley Grammar School moved to Rotherfield Court in 1928, when it became a County Council School. It also opened its doors to female students for the first time that year. In the years up until the Second World War, the number of students at the Grammar School dramatically increased; at the beginning of the War there were around 400 students attending HGS, nearly quadruple the number of boys at the school in 1922. Henley Grammar School now held a special place in the life of the town, educating generations of students. It had become 'A beacon light', as it was then described in the school hymn, both within Henley and in the minds of its students. Until the Education Act of 1944, HGS remained a fee-paying school, with the 1934 prospectus showing the fees to be £4 4s per term, including all books and stationery. The 11+ was introduced after the 1944 Education Act as a means of selection; it was replaced by the 13+ examination in 1966. There were serious local misgivings in Henley in 1972, when notice was given that education in south Oxfordshire would become comprehensive. In the wake of this reorganisation, Henley Grammar School stopped admitting younger pupils in 1974, who were accommodated in local 11-16 schools. The transition from Grammar School to Sixth Form College was finally completed in 1976.

HGS moved to an old manor house called Rotherfield Court in 1928. It had been built in 1861 for a Revd Dr Morrell, on a piece of land overlooking Henley called 'Ancastle'. Rotherfield Court was sold to the Makins family in 1872 and they enlarged both the house and the grounds. Rotherfield Court then contained a grand hall, library, billiard room, dining room and oak-panelled drawing room, shown to the left in a very rare photograph from the Makins family collection. The drawing room is now a staffroom at the present College.

Under the Makins, Rotherfield Court was a luxurious residence, a fact demonstrated by the mosaics which are still on display in the College's entrance area, previously the Old Hall at HGS. There was, however, only one fascination with the interior of the Court for Sir William Makins, who was raised at Rotherfield Court before the First World War. 'I was interested in seeing the organ in the hall', he told the HGS in 1967. 'This was worked by water-power and only "grown-ups" were allowed to touch it. However, when the opportunity came occasionally, my sisters and I would turn on the water to full power and try to find "The Great Amen" by each playing on a different part of the instrument at once.'

The greenhouses, photographed just before the school arrived in 1928, were reminders of life at Rotherfield under the Makins. 'As a boy,' wrote Sir William Makins of his childhood there, 'I had a passion for snakes and I can recall keeping one in the glass-house...and getting into trouble because the head gardener, who was terrified of them, refused to go into the glass-house for weeks after the snake – a harmless grass snake – had escaped.'

In 1921, Rotherfield Court was converted into a hospital for shell-shocked officers from the First World War, as Nannau Hospital in Wales was proving 'unsatisfactory' according to the Pensions Ministry. Rotherfield Court was fitted out to house fifty-one patients in thirty-two bedrooms, with each bedroom equipped with hot and cold water. The Pensions Ministry noted that 'The Mansion faces SE and occupies an elevated and sunny position, and is in this respect considered suitable for Neurasthenic patients.' The gardens were also full of interest for the patients. At this time there was still a tennis court, dutch garden, walled garden and an 'Old World' garden, as well as a fruit garden, kitchen garden, orchard and paddock. The Pensions Ministry were also pleased to note that the grounds contained a pig sty and cow shed.

A tank tower was built at Rotherfield Court in 1920, seen at the far left of this photograph. It contained a staircase and an electric passenger lift, so that the patients could be moved from one floor to another. The tower also housed a water tank, although the building was supplied by its own well. Tom Wheeler, later the school caretaker (see page 74), was initially employed to tend to the lift and the electrical generators and he long remembered his daily task of dragging gallons of water up from the well. The well ran dry in 1923 and from then the building was supplied with mains water.

The Opening Ceremony of HGS at Rotherfield Court was held in October 1928. It was led by the Lord Bishop of Oxford and concluded with a rendition of *God Save the King*, followed by tea. At first the boys and girls at HGS were still kept apart. They had separate apartments within the school, with the girls occupying the upper floor and the boys the lower. Huge iron gates also divided their playgrounds for the first few years at Rotherfield Court.

In the early days of HGS at Rotherfield there were two Common Rooms. The master's Common Room occupied what had once been an engine room, and Mr Clifford, a French teacher at the school from 1932 to 1969, remembered that it 'smelled vilely of oil'.

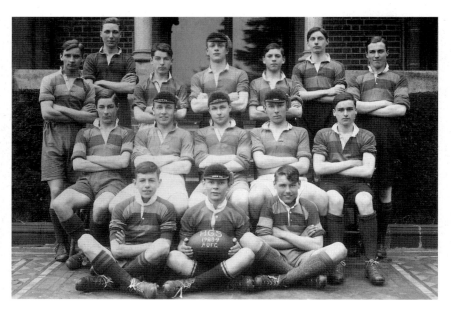

Five years before this photograph of the 1928-29 rugby team was taken, 'rugger' had replaced 'soccer' as the spring game at HGS. It had been reasoned in 1924 that by the middle of the preceding terms there had been flagging enthusiasm for football; much better, records *The Periam*, the 'Honest hard work and grit... peculiarly essential to Rugger.' 'But,' states the magazine, 'if this is British sport, why, no wonder we won the war!'

The front approach to Rotherfield Court from Paradise Road initially became the girls' drive, while the boys used the entrance from Pack and Prime Lane. Mr Clifford, the French teacher, remembered the following tale about these arrangements during the first few years of the school at Rotherfield: 'I was told by an Old Boy that for a brief period the girls used one drive, the boys another. This Old Boy celebrated the last day of his last term by choosing the most lovely girl in the school and walking with her down the drive.'

The 1930-31 rugby team had a 'winter of unparalleled success', praised *The Periam*, for 'The School has come through a gruelling season without defeat.' A.G. Butler, who later played rugby for England, is the captain sitting in the centre and, even before his later triumphs, his performance as full-back was hailed as 'exceptional in its brilliance'. Mr Williams (Uncle Bill), seen in the centre, was a geography teacher as well as a games coach. From left to right, back row: P. Prentice, H. Hope, D. Cox, S. Swan. Middle row: D. Boutell, J. Cook, B. Watt, Mr R. Williams, L. Elms, K. Kiddell, J. Willoughby. Front row: A. Cox, M. Smith, A.G. Butler, T. Cobb, G. Smith.

Above: HGS schoolgirls photographed during the early 1930s, soon after girls were first admitted to the school. Enid Austin is second girl on the left and all the girls are wearing their official school coats. Hilda Millicent Harding was also among the first intake of Grammar School girls and said that although no official mixing was allowed between boys and girls, who had separate playgrounds, staircases and corridors, the window on the girls' staircase proved very useful for passing notes and messages.

Right: Enid Austin in her HGS uniform, again photographed in the early 1930s. The uniform clearly suited Enid, but that was not always the case as the HGS teacher, Mr Clifford, remarked 'in those days any girl who looked the least comely was comely indeed, for their uniform was a gym-slip of the cruelest ugliness'.

The 1931 boys' cricket team was not the only squad playing the sport at HGS that year, for there were also attempts to set up a girls' cricket team. *The Periam*, however, laments that while the girls are 'keen' and many 'straight bats' have been discovered, bowling is proving a problem: 'it is inclined to make the game rather slow as the ball frequently fails to come within the batsmen's reach'.

HGS boys who gained their Rugby colours were allowed to wear special tasselled caps. George Francis's cap for the 1933–34 season is pictured to the left. Mr Francis was a student at the Grammar School from 1927 and recalls that discipline was then on old lines, whereby during the week, in every room, there was a list. 'You either got on a good list or a bad list', remembered Mr Francis. 'And if you got too many times on the bad list then Monday morning was the day of retribution, as it were.'

Left: Mr Soar was headmaster of HGS from 1931 to 1934, but during this short time he inspired many developments at the Grammar School. The iron gates separating the boys from the girls were taken down and under his leadership extra-curricular activities began to play an important role in school life. The Periam Society was set up under Mr Soar to 'advance debating and similar literary activities' within the Senior School. The Society's inaugural production was *Romeo and Juliet*, followed by *Hamlet* in 1934.

Below: Hamlet, pictured below in a very rare action shot, was directed by the Latin master, Mr Phillips. Miss Moss, the art mistress, designed the costumes. All the characters were dressed in black and white, apart from the players, who were clothed in fabulous colours. A whole term was spent making the costumes and the suits of armour were created from knitted dish cloth, which was then painted silver. The title role in the production was taken by S.J. Spackman and was, said the school magazine, 'an original interpretation, which would not have disgraced a professional actor'.

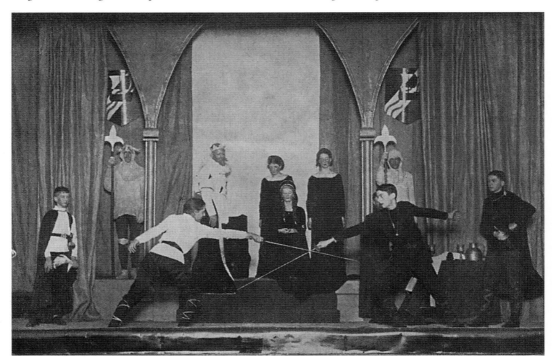

Right: The view of the gardens at Rotherfield in summer. The prospectus of 1935 tells parents that during the hotter months, cold drinks will be available at 11 a.m. and 1.15 p.m. in the dining room; hot milk and cocoa will be served at similar times in winter. It also states that 'Every pupil is required to bring at the beginning of each term a certificate of freedom from infectious diseases, signed by the parent or guardian.'

Below: The Old Boys of HGS formed the Old Henleiensians Association in 1922. Attempts had been made to create an Association before the First World War, but efforts were delayed by the hostilities. In August 1930 the Association formed the Old Henleiensians Rugby Club and one of their teams from the mid-1930s is pictured below. After a break during the war years, the Old Henleiensians Rugby Club was re-founded in 1954, changing its name to Henley RFC in 1963.

Initially girls' games at the newly coeducational school were hindered by lack of equipment, but it was not long before the school was making great advances in hockey and netball, as shown by this photograph of the hockey team from 1935.

The 1935 HGS cricket team all played for their various houses in the school tournament of that year. Valpy house emerged victorious, followed by Periam and Hambleden. Inter-house competition was not just the basis for sporting activities at HGS but also for cultural events. The judge of the 1936 inter-house music competition, Dr Armstrong, organist of Christ Church, Oxford, stressed to the three houses the importance of a 'realisation of their performers' limitations as well as their possibilities'.

A snapshot of form VA taken in 1936 on the terrace at Rotherfield. Three of the HGS boys pictured here lost their lives fighting in the Second World War.

The unpredictable English weather nearly stopped the 1937 tennis team proving their worth. 'Several matches at the beginning of the season had to be scratched owing to the rain', reported *The Periam*, 'but those played have all been won.' Perhaps the girls were inspired by new facilities for games at the school, for this season Mr Boniface made a 'new capacious cupboard' for the HGS girls' sports gear.

The headmaster, H.D. Barnes, seated at the centre of the 1937 school prefects, often had an unorthodox outlook on his role. His study was above the prefects' room and on one occasion the students below were making too much noise, throwing a ball against the wall. Barnes expressed his disapproval by banging on the floor. After they had been quiet for a few minutes, the prefects saw something falling past their window. It was a bag of buns thrown down by Barnes in appreciation of their silence.

Miss Ishbell Macdonald distributing prizes at HGS Speech Day in October 1937. The Mayor of Henley also often paid an annual visit to the school at this time of year. His visits were always well received by the students, as he would ask the headmaster to grant a half-holiday to mark the occasion.

The school prefects from 1938, with H.D. Barnes, the headmaster, and Miss Hunter, senior mistress, seated in the centre. Miss Hunter had just returned from the United States when this photograph was taken, as she had been teaching there during 1936–37; she had taken up an exchange post with Dr Rees of Alhambra City High School, California. Miss Hunter was a well-liked and respected member of staff, described as a woman of admirable high standards.

The rugby team of 1938-39 were a 'new and rather inexperienced pack' according to the school magazine, but they still managed to win half their matches. Mr Potter, the senior mathematics and games master, stands at the centre of the back row. Potter had joined HGS in 1937, leaving three years later to serve in the Navy. After his ship was sunk in 1942, he spent three years as a POW in the Far East. He returned to HGS after the War and was remembered as 'a man who stimulated the efforts of the abler pupils and by his quiet efficiency, thoroughness and kindness, gave confidence to the weaker'.

The HGS photograph albums from 1929 through to 1956 still exist. They mainly contain images of various school sports teams, yet among such athletic shots are these unusual images from 1939, showing the Grammar School boys being taught how to cook fish.

The hockey team of 1939–1940 were not able to play many of their matches that term due to 'transport and other war difficulties', states *The Periam*.

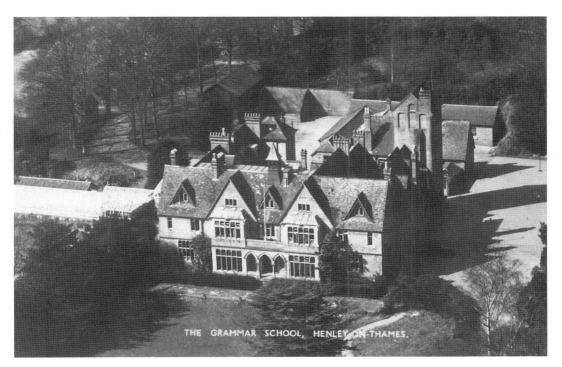
THE GRAMMAR SCHOOL, HENLEY ON-THAMES.

From 1939 until the summer of 1941, Henley Grammar School shared its premises with 200 evacuees from North Kensington Central School. The arrangements were that the Henley pupils would attend from 8.45 a.m. to 12.55 p.m. for 'ordinary schooling' and from 2 p.m. to 3.15 p.m. for games and practical subjects. North Kensington scholars attended school from 1.30 p.m. to 4.15 p.m., except on Wednesdays when the school was closed for cleaning; a break which would be compensated for on Saturday mornings. From 1941 until Easter 1953, the Grammar School welcomed the pupils of the Royal Alexandra School, Bishop's Wood. These students were affectionately known as the 'Camp People' and became part of school life at the Grammar School, even providing the school with a head girl, Edith Biggin, from their numbers (1942-43).

Mr Barnes was headmaster at HGS from 1934 to 1957, leading the school throughout the difficult war years; at one time, only Miss Hunter and Miss Wilkinson remained of the school's original staff. Barnes kept a diary of life at the school throughout this period, and so recorded the beginning of the autumn term at the Grammar School in 1940: 'Term began today. Started with prayers, followed by air raid drill ... Read psalm (9:15) of "terror that flieth by night" at prayers as seemed very appropriate.'

The memorial plaque for those who fell in the Second World War was almost identical to one which commemorated losses from HGS in the First World War. The Roll of Honour, pictured to the right, includes W. Bryant, a history teacher from the Grammar School. *The Periam* remembered that 'Shortly before he left England he remarked that he had always spoken and worked against Fascism and now it was time to fight it.' He was killed in 1945 during the Anglo-US offensive to capture Geilenkirchen.

The grounds had begun to return to their former glory by the autumn of 1946. Not only is the 'last trace of shagginess gone from our yew hedge', praised *The Periam*, but 'the playing fields begin to look as once we knew them; the fine lawns of which we are so proud are again acquiring their former trimness.'

The post-war rugby team photographed in 1946. Boys' games suffered during the War, with *The Periam* recording that 'At one particularly difficult period Rugby, Football and Cricket had to be organised and supervised by one master.' The return of Mr Potter, as maths and games master in 1946, instilled a new 'fierce purposefulness' into rugby and cricket at the school.

Right: Hockey at HGS soon recovered from war deprivations with the 1945-46 team enjoying a good season, conceding only one defeat and winning four of their matches. From left to right, back row: M. Dyer, -?-, Miss Broadbent, M. Tomalin, P. Simpson. Middle row: F. Cripps, J. Devereux, C. Muir, J. Davis, M. Barnes. Front row: S. Clarke.

Below: The 1946 HGS cricket team. From left to right, back row: Hyman, Clark, R. Wood, A. Moore, P. Walters, Sawbridge. Middle row: Saunders, P. Loosley, I. Scott, G. Russell, E. Ellis. Front row: M. Scott, J. Tarry.

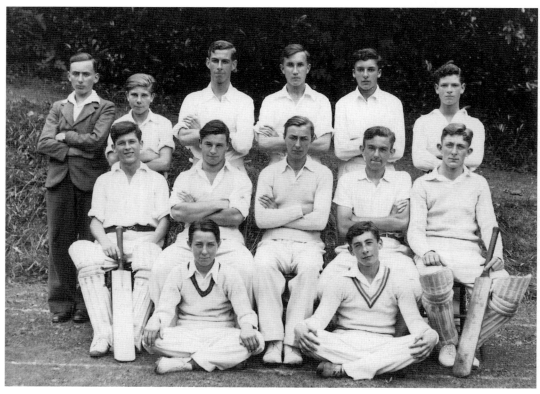

Left: Mary Clarke, *née* Barnes, was HGS head girl in 1946 and is photographed here in the girls' winter uniform. Mary Clarke later became Secretary to the Henley Educational Charity, which was initially formed in 1944 as a Foundation Trust, to use money from the school's ancient endowments to provide scholarships to the Grammar School. Henley Educational Charity still exists today and has a general charitable interest in education in Henley.

Below: The senior prefects photographed in 1946. From left to right, back row: A. Moore, M. Barnes, G. Wickens, J. Flecknoe, M. Day. Front row: P. Loosley, E. Heath, H.D. Barnes, C. Muir, J. Devereux. H.D. Barnes, the headmaster, was known to colleagues and students as 'Sam' from his fondness for reading extracts from Dickens' *The Pickwick Papers*, which included a famous imitation of Sam Weller.

Above: The school play of 1947, *Lady Precious Stream*, was produced by Miss Cunnington, pictured here on the far left of the back row. Miss Cunnington began teaching at HGS in 1944 and a year later had overseen a school production of *Noah*, the old medieval play. As this was just after the War, the animal costumes were all made out of defunct blackout material. The actors had processed across the lawn at Rotherfield, stopping on the terrace, where they sang a penitential psalm. 'God' had been positioned on the balcony above and, after the psalm, turned on a hose-pipe, thus beginning his flood. Noah then sent off a raven, tied onto a rope attached to the mast-head, and afterwards did the same for a dove. 'God' from his vantage point in the balcony clipped an olive branch to the dove and sent it back to Noah, to the thanksgiving of all below. From left to right, back row: Miss Cunnington, B. Wilson, M. Glover, Johnson, P. Tucker, A. Miller, A. Hobbs, E. Ellis. Middle row: S. Smith, R. Clayton, M. Dyer, M. Day, B. Tarry, F. Albon, M. Holder, A. Moore, J. Andrew. Front row: R. Sainsbury, I. Scott, -?-, A. Miller.

Opposite above: The girls' tennis VI of 1947 were an unbeaten side. From left to right, back row: F.L. Cripps, M.E. Bean. Front row: P.A. Simpson, M. Handford, J.S. Flecknoe, N.J. Davies.

Opposite below: A rare photograph of two Grammar School boys carrying out a drag experiment, captured in the school magazine in the summer of 1947.

Right: Headmaster H.D. Barnes, standing at the centre of the 1947 prefects, apparently used to refer to the sixth formers as 'The Cream of the Cream', whereas the lower school were on occasion referred to as 'Bottomless wells of abysmal ignorance'. From left to right, back row: -?-, M. Glover, Miss Hunter, H.D. Barnes, Potter, A. Moore. Front row: M. Dyer, J. Dixon, J. Flecknoe, G. Wickens, M. Day. P Loosley.

The HGS hockey team of 1946-47. From left to right, back row: Audrey Miller, Sheena Grierson, Margaret Handford, Molly Stoner, Jean Barlow, Helen Watts. Front row: Pat Simpson, Jean Davies, Freda Cripps, Mavis Dyer, Phyllis Mills. Audrey Rooks, *née* Miller, on the far left back row also remembers taking part in swimming lessons at HGS. The pool at this time was merely a roped-off part of the Thames and Audrey remembers walking back, ravenously hungry, buying cakes which then had to be hidden under their Panama hats whenever the staff were nearby.

Milton's *Comus*, again produced by Miss Cunnington, was performed on the terrace in front of the school in June 1948. The animal masks were created by Geoff Makins, the art master.

A special overture for the 1949 school production of *The Rivals*, was written by F.G. Alborn and played by the school orchestra. Produced by Miss Cunnington, it was performed in the Old Hall at the school and once again, Mr Makins was responsible for the scenery.

The prefects of 1950, with Audrey Rooks (*née* Miller) photographed on the back row on the far left. She remembers that the prefects at this time would save up their 'morning milk' and would use it to make 'camp coffee' after school.

Reginald Brind was the excellent music master at HGS from 1941 until 1969. Mr Brind initially shared his teaching time with Chiltern Edge School, but as music was extended at HGS he became a permanent fixture in the school. The choir and orchestra flourished under Mr Brind and the annual carol concert, together with performances at Speech Day and in the summer, never failed to delight all those present.

The crucial match of the season, which pitted the 1951 HGS cricket team against the Old Henleiensians, the Old Boys team, was disappointingly declared a draw after bad light stopped play.

An impromptu photograph of Form 4A from the Grammar School, taken on the lawn at Rotherfield in July 1951.

Above: The Old Henleians Hockey Club was set up in 1947 by Old Girls of the Grammar School who wanted to continue playing hockey. This soon became a mixed club and during the summer months the Old Henleians Hockey Club became a tennis club. In 1951 a group from the club decided to organise a trip to the French Riviera. They overhauled an old bus, which they named *Effort*, and even incorporated built-in running water. Here is the party photographed in Henley on their return from France. The group included Mary Barnes, Robert Berry, Jeanette Bowles, John Bowles, Robert Brackston, Tom Broad, Ken Clarke, June Compton, Gwen Davies, Joan Fenton, Betty Foreman, Des Huppler, Sylvia Morris, Vera Russell, Gordon Russell, 'Spenny' Seymour, Beryl and Sidney Swan, John Tarry, Ron Wood. On their return from France the Old Henleians Hockey Club was renamed Henley Hockey Club.

Opposite above: Henry IV Part I was the school production of 1951 and the reviewer in *The Periam* noted that 'On leaving the Hall after a performance, I heard [an unknown member of 2A] say "Gosh, it was just as good as a real play".'

Opposite below: An action shot from the 1951 production of *Henry VI Part I*. The play was performed in the Old Hall of the Grammar School, which is now the reception area in the College's Rotherfield building. The Old Hall was quite a restricted space and the fight scenes had to be carefully choreographed. To prevent any untimely accidents, the lights at the front of stage were covered in chicken wire.

Brilliant, warm weather ensured that 1952 was a good year for athletics at the school. Ten records were broken at the school Sports Day that year and Harman came third in the mile at the Army Cadet Finals; his time of 4 minutes 40 seconds was, at the time, the best ever recorded by an HGS boy.

The photograph of the HGS netball team of 1953 fails to express the difficult existence netball often had at the school. 'Enthusiasm for netball dies an early death in this School', lamented *The Periam* over twenty years before in 1931, 'therefore few people can ever realise what an excellent game it is'. 'Girls who go on to college,' the writer adds in warning, 'will find that netball has as many aspirants for positions in the teams as hockey.'

The cast of the school production of *As You Like It*, from Easter 1953. Mr Attrill, the geography teacher, appeared in the production at short notice as Jacques, after the previous actor was indisposed, undertaking to learn all his lines in three days. From left to right, back row: Lait, M. Reeves, G. Miller, Smith, Roberts, Mr Attrill, Giles, A. Griggs, Griggs, Nunn, P. Smith, Kinchin. Front row: J. Martin, Griffin, B. Williams, Hewlett, C. Smith, Thomas, Rixon, Rider.

Some of the Lower Sixth from HGS, photographed in 1953 on a trip to Silbury Mound, Avebury. From left to right: R. Killick, D. Hughes, D. Cobb, L. Lait, D. Colyer.

Above: The cast of *Iphigenia in Tauris* photographed on the terrace at Rotherfield. This was the school production of summer 1953 and was attended by John Masefield, the poet laureate, and his wife. Masefield afterwards wrote to Miss Cunnington, the producer, to congratulate all involved with the production. Miss Cunnington wrote back to say that it was a pity that he had not been shown to his seat by one Mr Attrill, the geography teacher at the school; Mr Attrill had seated most of the audience, yet the headmaster had acted as guide for the Masefields, the guests of honour. Miss Cunnington's point was that if Masefield had been greeted by Mr Attrill, he would then have met the man she was to marry. Much to their surprise, Masefield then wrote a letter to Mr Attrill, apologising for not being able to meet him at the performance and congratulating him on his forthcoming marriage.

Opposite above: The school decorations for the Queen's Coronation in 1953 were designed by Mr Makins, the art master. There was a special service in the School Hall to celebrate the Coronation, where a string orchestra accompanied the organ. Every member of the sixth form wore a buttonhole, presented by the headmaster, Mr Barnes.

Opposite below: In the autumn of 1953, Princess Margaret planted the first tree of the Coronation Avenue in the Fair Mile. The whole of HGS was present for the ceremony and the headmaster, Mr Barnes, was presented to Princess Margaret.

The Chemistry and Physics Laboratory at the school was captured in *The Periam* in 1954. 'Old Henleiensians', stated the magazine, 'will be interested to note the fluorescent lighting and the new arrangement of benches.'

The 1954-55 HGS rugby team won six of their eight matches, even severely testing the Old Henleiensians, for the 'School pack... outclassed the heavier Old Henleiensians' forwards'. Although the match was eventually won by the Old Boys, the HGS team still declared it their 'best performance' of the season.

The cast of the 1954 school production, *A Midsummer Night's Dream*, were assembled in a thankfully dry moment, in what proved a year of 'chaotic weather', according to the school magazine. The play was produced by Mrs Attrill, with Peter Thomas as Oberon, Jean Washbrook as Titania, supported by Derek Giles as Bottom and Brian Hewlett as Puck.

Puck, on the far right of the photograph, was played by Brian Hewlett. After leaving HGS, Brian became a professional actor, playing Amos Hart in the first West End production of *Chicago*. For many years he has been the voice of Neil Carter in the Radio 4 serial, *The Archers*.

The HGS prefects from 1954–55. Mrs Clayden, who taught at HGS for thirteen years, is seated in the centre next to H.D Barnes, the headmaster. Mrs Clayden took over from Miss Hunter as senior mistress and was described by one as 'strict but at the same time quite motherly'. From left to right, back row: D. Hughes, M. Reeves, J. Martin, D. Colyer. Front row: G. Miller, L. Lait, H.D. Barnes, M. Clayden, A. Griggs, R. Roberts.

A school garden was destroyed in 1954 to make room for the new biology laboratory, seen here a year later. Before that Miss Wilkinson had presided over biology in the attics at Rotherfield. 'If', recorded the magazine, 'the old laboratory in the roof could produce so many able biologists, agriculturalists and doctors, how great are the potentials of the new one?'

This photograph of HGS pupils taking a morning stroll along the Seine was taken during the Easter trip to Paris in 1955. While the boys were sipping drinks in one of the French cafés, the girls deserted them in favour of the shops. A newspaper photographer spotted them later walking by the Seine and photographed them in their school caps. The next evening the boys appeared in *France Soir*.

During the 1955 trip the HGS girls spent some time browsing in the stalls on the banks of the Seine. According to P. Thomas writing of the trip in the school magazine, 'although the people were friendly to us, their idea of politeness did not always conform to our own'.

'As in previous years', lamented *The Periam* in the summer of 1956, 'the first three weeks of term found everyone busy training for school sports, and little practice with bat and ball was seen on the school field. It came as no surprise therefore, when the school only managed 35 in their first match.' Performances soon improved with the team, under their 'audacious leader' Stolarow, hitting 138 for 9 against Slough and turning in a good performance against the Old Boys. The team included, in no particular order: Stolarow, Kernick, Tristem, Wood, Bathgate, Owen, Castle, Mears, Pike, Waller, Platt, Allwright.

The 1957–58 HGS rugby 1st XV. From left to right, back row: A. Farmer, M. Kernick, P. Mayers, N. Younger, M. Jones, D. Teasdale, M. Kernick, A. Platt, R. Hillier. Front row: A. Austin, P. Bennett, R. Waller, M. Owen (capt.), B. Lucas, D. Pearson-Kirk, P. Davies.

The School Cadet Force, which was formed during Mr Valpy's headmastership, was granted CCF status by the War Office in 1958, the year this photograph was taken. The Cadets were allowed more time for their weekly parade and to attend CCF camps, where they would meet cadets from other schools.

The 1st tennis VI of 1958, consisting of L. Roberts as captain, together with D. Farmer, H. Wilczek, S. Crocker, A. Read and J. Smith, was a strong team, as all were members of the previous year's 1st VI. All had earned their colours and indeed the team was now so strong that the school magazine lamented that 'some of the opponents the team met were unable to extend our players or give sufficient rallies to allow couples to advance to the net'.

The 1st hockey XI of 1957–58 was also captained by L. Roberts, who played alongside J. Wadley, S. Crocker, H. Wilczek, G. Smith, L. Bushell, J. Oscroft, H. Grimshaw, D. Edwards, D. Farmer, and P. Grattan. From the Easter of 1958, boys' hockey was regularly being played at the school, under Mr Martyn.

Right: HGS boys inspecting a cannon on a school trip to Blenheim Palace in 1958. From left to right: A. Smith, C. Thompson, I. Gilbert, N. Hill, R. Parker. Robert Parker was one of three students visiting the Grammar School from the USA.

Below: The HGS athletics team from the summer of 1958. From left to right, back row: D. Martin, A. Austin, D. Crabbe, D. Lewis, R. Drury, P. Mayers, P. Latham, C. Bird. Front row: R. Walker, N. Younger, D. Pearson-Kirk, P. Davies, B. Lucas (capt), M. Owen, D. Teasdale, A. Farmer.

The prefects of 1958–59, with Mr Lipscomb, the headmaster, seated in the centre. After taking over from H.D. Barnes in 1957, Lipscomb ran the school until 1966. He was described by the school magazine as a 'doughty fighter'. Lipscomb's final years at HGS were characterised by national discussion over secondary reorganisation, yet he continued to believe passionately in the mission of Grammar Schools in the country. On the left of Lipscomb sits Clem Clifford, deputy head, with Vera Paul, the senior mistress, on the right.

HGS pupils on a school trip at Easter 1959 were photographed by an Italian newspaper photographer walking down the steps of the Capitoline Hill in Rome. Those visible, from left to right: S. Stephenson, L. Lester, J. Hague, J. Kass, J. Robbins, K. Rose, M. Brooks, E. Burgess, -?-. Noel Younger, head boy at HGS from September of that year, noted in his photograph album of the trip that the boys became very acquainted with the fountain outside the girls' pension in Rome, for they 'had to wait there for the girls (every time we went out!) until they were ready'.

The 1959-60 HGS rugby VII. The team had a brilliant run of success in the Oxford Sevens Tournament that year, making it through to the semi-finals before being knocked out by Haberdashers Askes. From left to right, back row: P. Mayers, N. Younger, M. Kernick, N. Hougham, P. Jones. Front row: G. Motyka, T. Austin, A. Farmer.

This photograph of HGS pupils was taken in 1960 in the Square of the Capitol in Rome, during the 'Continental Tour' of that year. The group visited Belgium, Germany, Austria and Italy. In Venice the boys stayed in a monastery and the girls in a convent, and they had the first cappuccino in St Mark's Square. By the end of their trip, however, Jacqueline Lee wrote 'by now I was longing...to drink something that was not coffee or Coca-Cola, preferably tea'.

The HGS rugby 1st XV from 1960-61. Mr Lipscomb is seated in the centre and Mr Rees, the games master, is standing on the far left, back row. Wally Rees, who was also in charge of CCF activities in the school, proved one of the school's enduring great characters. 'A man full of wit and Welsh ebullience', described *The Periam*, 'who could make an ordinary sentence sound like oratory'.

Membership of the HGS boatclub had doubled by 1962 and they had their first chance of forming a third IV. Interest in rowing had a long precedent at the school. Back in 1925 a debate was held on the motion that 'Boat-racing is an artificial and much over-rated sport'. It was defeated by nine votes to two.

The new headmaster of HGS, David Henschel, sits in the middle of the 1966 school cricket team. Henschel had taken over as headmaster from Lipscomb at the beginning of the summer term. The previous summer an appeal had been made for more girls to help with games teas, calling those who were able to 'inconspicuously remove plates and mugs before the teams have finished eating out of them (or preferably before they have started). This strategy is to prevent their lingering too long (when you want to get home to watch *Juke Box Jury*).'

A stall at the school fête of July 1966. Mr Rees' management of the summer fête was masterful, according to the HGS magazine: 'Shall we ever forget the way he ran the summer fête? Standing on the terrace, his runners at his side, his head thrown back, a gleam in his eye, he reminded one of an old-time commander in the field.'

Tom Wheeler, the caretaker for over forty years, was one of the great characters of HGS. Headmasters and staff might have come and gone, but Tom was a integral presence at HGS and few Old Boys would return to the school without seeking him out. He would remember them all, even if they had left the school thirty years before. 'He was indeed a man of infinite resource', wrote Clem Clifford, 'infinite patience and splendidly unperturbed in an emergency. When others shouted, he spoke gently, when others foretold disaster, he would quietly think out a solution to the problem.'

The school's Amateur Radio Project took their equipment to Henley Regatta in 1970 and made 400 contacts with other stations around the country. 'We hope', stated the group, 'that the public are now more aware of the presence of amateur radio in the electronic age we live in.'

The school's Charity Walk of 1970 was entered by 123 volunteers and they each covered eighteen miles.

The Upper Sixth photographed in the summer of 1971. Several members of the year represented the Grammar School at a Sixth Form Conference held that summer at Jesus College, Oxford. 'In the afternoons, most people could be found on the river', wrote the sixth formers of their experience, 'or alternatively in the river depending on how hot it was or how good their punting!'

Right: Much Ado About Nothing, the school production of 1971. The cast were hit with 'flu the week of the production but *The Periam* records that 'despite sore throats, streaming eyes and heavy heads, the play was a great success'. From left to right: Lynne Irwin, Jane Murrell, Sharon Miller and Alison Bath.

Below: The 1974 Upper Sixth photographed with their teachers. The school regulations of that year contained the following warning for boys: 'Please see that hair is within the following revised lengths, above the eyebrows at the front, not below the jaw at the side, not over the collar, and that it is clean and tidy. Boys who break the new regulation will have to return to it, to the letter.' Henley Grammar School was to close two years later.

four

'Come questioning,
go seeking, grow'
1976–1987

King James's College of Henley

King James's Sixth Form College was established in Henley in 1976. In many ways the College grew out of the tradition established by Henley Grammar School, as it was named after the founder of the Grammar School and occupied the same buildings at Rotherfield. Yet there were also many necessary developments which heralded this new institution; uniform was abolished and the new College would now accommodate around 800 students. In its eleven short years, Oxfordshire's only sixth form college gained a considerable reputation not only locally, but also nationally. The words of the College motto 'Come Questioning, Go Seeking, Grow' were embraced by many who studied at King James's College and it became a centre of cultural, as well as academic achievement. The increasingly close relationship with the South Oxfordshire Technical College culminated in their union in 1987, but there was great sadness at the closure of King James's College. Keith Dawson, the last principal of the College, remarked that King James's had experienced 'a bright life' and that during its short existence 'the College has been dedicated to the pursuit of excellence and wholehearted participation, not only in academic work, but also in the physical, cultural and social activities without which education, properly understood, cannot exist'.

Students from King James's College, sitting on the lawn outside the Rotherfield buildings.

It was the first principal of the college, David Henschel, headmaster of the Grammar School since 1966, who secured permission from Her Majesty the Queen to name the college after its original founder, James I, so ensuring that links with the past were maintained. Another tradition which survived the transition from grammar school to sixth form college was the annual pilgrimage to St Mary's Church for the Dame Periam Service. In later years, Henschel changed this to Founders' Day to commemorate all those involved with the College's history, for which he wrote a Founders' Day Prayer. David Henschel is pictured above with his wife Norah, outside St Mary's Church on Founders' Day.

All pupils and staff would attend the annual Founders' Day service, the latter resplendent in their academic gowns and hoods, afterwards filing past Dame Periam's tomb in the church.

The victorious 1977 girls' junior IV crew at Nottingham City Regatta. From left to right: S. Mills, G. Seymour, A. Churchill, F. Pamplin, K. Lacey. King James's College always took a keen interest in rowing, especially after the arrival of Elly Scantlebury as coach in 1979.

Sally Dexter, pictured here with Clive Preston as Bottom, gave a remarkable performance as Titania in the College's 1978 production of *A Midsummer Night's Dream*. The following year she appeared as Lady Macbeth in another KJC production, a role she was later to return to with the National Youth Theatre. Sally Dexter has gone on to have a very successful acting career, winning an Olivier award for her work.

The victorious 1st rugby XV of 1978. From left to right, back row: Chris Emerson, Simon Kelly, Pete Rice, Russell Challis, Huw Jones, Kevin Hurst, Greg Kent, Matthew Blundell, Geoff Lehey, Jeremy Goldwyn. Front row: Brian Anderson, Mike Jennings, Jon Allen, Chris Grey, John Horne.

Equus was the second production of the King James's Players, which was a company of staff, students and parents created by the principal, David Henschel, who directed its first production of *Twelfth Night*. The 1979 production, directed by English teacher Peter Allen, was the amateur première of the controversial play by Peter Schaffer and ran for a week at the Kenton Theatre in 1979 to sell-out houses. Peter Cockman in the centre played Dysart, Celia Hemken to the left played Jill and Julian Waite played Alan Strang.

The cast of *Superkist*, an original rock musical written by Peter Allen, an English teacher at KJC; the music was composed by David Arch, a student at the College, who went on to be musical director for many West End musicals. This was premièred in 1980 for the College Arts Festival. From left to right: David Penrose, Robert Simpson, Andrea Bull, Willem Postema, Daniel Booker, Kris Baron, Clare Charles, Simon Marlow. Front row: Yaron Levy.

One highlight of the third KJC Arts Festival in 1981 was the Jazz, Folk and Blues evening, which attracted up to five local and student bands. The photograph shows the student band The Stills performing on stage in Rotherfield Hall.

Right: The poet John Cooper Clark appeared at the Poetry and Beer Evening in the College Arts Festival of 1981. Previous festivals had witnessed performances from other poets including Roger McGough and Gavin Ewart. John Cooper Clark, a contentious punk poet from Salford, brought the house down with his witty and irreverent humour.

Below: Linton Kwesi Johnson performed on a double bill with John Cooper Clark at the Poetry and Beer Evening. The hall was packed for this controversial evening and it was the first time Clark and Johnson had appeared on stage together.

The award-winning cast of *Popsy Bananas* at the Kenton Drama Festival in 1981. The show was written by English teacher Peter Allen with music by student David Arch and choreography by the company. It was one of the few musicals ever to enter the Festival. From left to right: Rachel Head, Alexis Hurst, Caroline Seed and Sophie Yeates. The College won the Youth Award six times between 1980 and 1987 and the Stage Director's Trophy in 1983.

A staff and student production in 1982 of the Italian comedy of *Saturday Sunday Monday* by Filippo. From left to right, back row: Sarah Gerrard, John Grace, Jonathan Godfrey, Dave Ferraro and producer John Davies. Front row: Raymonde Nathan, Peter Allen, Linzi Owen, Joan Clark, Anne Davies, Martin Dew.

The house system from HGS days continued at the new College, with students still divided into Hambleden, Periam or Valpy. Although the idea superficially appeared old-fashioned within the modern College, it helped promote a sense of belonging to KJC. P13, one of the Periam forms, is photographed with their tutor, Andy Pegg, in September 1982. From left to right, back row: A. King, R. Hotton, S. Finch, P. Aikens, D. Willis, A. Taylor, M. Gillard, P. Mummery, N. Ralf, A. Pegg. Front row: S. Chesterton, C. Nicholson, S. Lloyd, F. Burns, C. Methven, P. Cornwall, M. Gambrill.

The cast of the 1982 KJC production of *Cinders* by Glowacki. It initially premièred at the Royal Court Theatre, after which the College gained permission to perform it with the original script. From left to right: C. Stewart, R. Seymour, T. Chaffer, J. Flynn, A. McCarthy and C. James.

There were many inter-house competitions at KJC, with almost all students participating in some capacity, even if only in the massed house choir. Form P11, one of the Periam forms from 1982, is photographed with their tutor, Peter Allen. The first year are seated in the front, with the second year standing behind. From left to right, back row: K. Selway, C. Cotton, R. Lovett, J. Charles, R. Elvin, P. Allen, B. Quilty, D. Scott, P. Jeffery, S. Gerrard, J. Duckmanton. Front row: N. Milborrow, L. Daly, S. Parr, S. Kirby, C. Thompson, P. Newell, F. Walker.

A scene from the 1983 KJC production of *The Crucible* by Arthur Miller, with Charlotte du Sautoy on the left together with Mike Seares.

The staff of King James's College on the front lawn. From left to right, back row: Peter Allen, Tony Chanter, Ian Wainwright, Gerry Baker, Mike Gibby, Alan Jenkins, Gareth Rowlands, Iain Johnstone, David Henschel, Steve Owen, David Mitchell, Graham Horner, Chris Walker, Stan Isherwood, Julie Lane, David Ferraro, Hywel Thomas, Kay Szebeny. Middle row: Steve Hawker, Brenda Percy, Debbie Bacon, Margaret Day, Geraldine Evans, Allan Jones, Anne Davies, Jean Ede, Olga Sheen, Norah Henschel. Front row: Mary Beckinsale, Glyn James, Isobel Cisneros, Rhoda Cope, Joyce Green, Joan Clark, Rene Cleverly, Ann Cole, Gill Davies, Alison Buxston.

Leading members of the cast of *Once in a Lifetime* by Kaufman and Hart. Make up was specially created by Rudi Kartal for the period and the show ran for a week at the Kenton Theatre in 1984, the first of several cooperative ventures between the College and the management of the theatre. From left to right, back row: J. Baird, V. Simpson, C. du Sautoy, J. Marsh, D. Tidley. Front row: C. Bower, A. Moss.

Keith Dawson, principal at King James from 1984 to 1987, with Rhoda Cope, College Librarian, inside the new Library built in 1985. Rhoda Cope led a group of professional librarians that were determined, in spite of often difficult physical conditions within the College, that their library should form a training ground for higher education. Stock was greatly increased by private efforts, especially those of the '1604 Club'. Founded and organised by Brian Diplock, later Judith Payne, it was promoted in College by Stephen Hawker and Ian Johnstone. Together with their band of volunteers, mostly mothers, they provided the extra assistance the library vitally needed.

Right: Fashion shows, such as the one on the right, were organised for many years by The College Association to raise funds for KJC. The College Association developed out of the Grammar School PTA, but the new College decided to broaden its scope, involving all past and present parents, staff and pupils. Fashion shows, Victorian evenings, horse shows and auctions were not only very profitable but hugely enjoyable parts of life at King James's College.

Below: A Midsummer Night's Dream was the College's ambitious first European drama tour in 1986. The venture took a full-scale production, with fifty students and crew, first to Leichlingen near Koln, Henley's twin town, and then on to Munich to a huge theatre venue. The company then moved into communist Czechoslovakia and performed first in Karlovy Vary and then just outside Prague. The final performance was back in Germany at Grevenbroich in the Rhineland.

Left: The award-winning group who won a network of brand new Apricot computers in 'The Sunday Times Domesday 1000 Competition' of 1986. The group prepared their entry for an English project and they are photographed with their teacher Joan Clark. The competition was for all schools in the country to imagine their own community in 2086, 1000 years after the original Domesday Book. One of the judges, the Science Editor of *The Sunday Times*, had expected science students to be the winners and was amazed to learn they were English students. The group received their award from the Queen Mother in the Great Hall at Winchester.

Below: The College annually staged an opera and *La Belle Hélène* was the choice of 1986. The operas were directed by Christopher Walker and David Ferraro and they managed to inspire tremendous enthusiasm among a cast and crew of 200. For many students the annual opera, and the obligatory opera party, remained their enduring memory of their time at KJC.

Above: Students enjoying the last Summer Ball in 1987, an integral part of the year at KJC. The ball was often associated with the Arts Festivals, but it was also seen as an art form in its own right. Gill Davies and Peter Allen spent many years overseeing these spectacular events, and the principal Keith Dawson wrote that they 'through style, elegance, enthusiasm and wholehearted enjoyment somehow conjured up an Oxford Summer Ball for about a fiver'. From left to right: A. Cornish, P. Wright, G. Storch, A. Davies.

Right: Keith Dawson, the last principal of KJC, photographed on Founders' Day standing on the front lawn of the College before the procession of staff and students left for the church service. Dawson summed up the feelings of many on the passing of the College: 'It is a matter of regret – the passing of King James's. But on the other hand, the potential of the new college is enormous and if it is done right, it should be a very exciting place to work and be.'

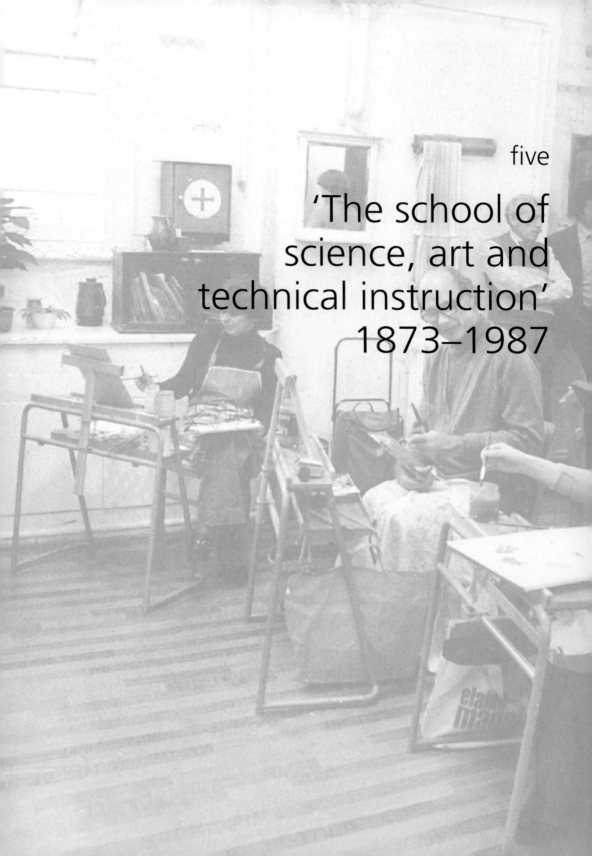

five

'The school of
science, art and
technical instruction'
1873–1987

The Technical College

Henley's 'School of Science and Art and Technical Instruction' was founded in Hart Street in 1873, but by the end of the nineteenth century it was situated in Duke Street. Emily Climeson's *Guide to Henley-on-Thames*, published in 1896, notes that subjects taught at the Institute included 'drawing, magnetism, electricity, shorthand, theoretical and practical chemistry, elementary mathematics, book-keeping &c'. Fees that year were 2s 6d a session. By 1916 the Technical Institute's annual budget was £185 yet all of its staff remained part-time. The fortunes of the Technical Institute began to swiftly improve after the 1944 Education Act and responsibility for the Institute transferred to Oxfordshire County Council in 1948. A few years later, in 1953, it was decided that the Institute needed a full-time principal and should acquire permanent premises.

The site of the old Henley Liberal Club in the Reading Road housed the Institute for a few years but it soon proved too small. In 1959 it was therefore decided that the Institute should move to the former buildings of Henley Secondary Modern School on Gravel Hill. Just before the move the Institute was renamed as the 'South Oxfordshire Technical College' and the College opened its doors on Gravel Hill in 1962. The Technical College remained on that site, with ever increasing numbers of students, until its amalgamation with King James's College in 1987.

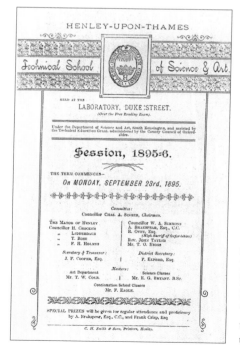

A prospectus still exists from the 1895-6 session at the Technical Institute. The details of the science curriculum include the following enticement: 'In order to secure increased interest in these Classes... the Teacher shall have the assistance of a powerful lime-light magic lantern to convey to the mind of the student a clearer perception of the subject under consideration. No effort will be spared to make the subjects interesting as well as instructive.' An Industrial and Artistic Exhibition was also organised by the Institute in 1899. Categories included the best home-made hive and the best-made nightdress. 'Marks will be awarded,' the programme warned, 'for the excellence of the needlework, not for a highly trimmed garment.'

From the end of the nineteenth century to 1953, the Institute was housed in Duke Street. For many years, on the floor below, there was a Free Reading Room where 'A number of newspapers, general and local, and periodicals are to be seen here free; the hours are from 9 a.m. to 10 p.m., Wednesdays 12 a.m. to 10 p.m.'

The Technical Institute moved in 1953 to the former premises of the Henley Liberal Club in Reading Road; the building which later housed 'Champions', the ironmongers. It then gained its first full-time member of staff, the principal Mr Roland Wilcock. He remembered that when the Institute first moved to Reading Road 'the place was being fitted out and I had to use the Congregational Church Hall as a base. I kept all my papers and enrolment forms in the back of my car!' The Institute at that time contained 'a well-equipped engineering workshop, a carpentry and joinery shop, a laboratory, a drawing office and a lecture room for commercial subjects'.

The Institute curriculum after it had moved to the Reading Road included book binding and shoe repairing, shown above. Both of these courses took place in the cellar. The Institute caused a furore in 1955, recorded by the *Henley Standard*, for the course 'Women's woodwork – repeat, woodwork! – outnumbered, and judged by what was seen, also rivalled in quality, the work of the men!'

The Technical College moved to the old site of the National School, later Henley Secondary Modern School, during 1960-61. The principal then, Mr Wilcock, together with architect Julian Leathart, had to redesign the interior. 'There was no interior circulation then,' he explained, 'You had to go outside from each classroom – there were no corridors. And the headmaster's house was still buried in there.' The old central staircase was therefore removed and two modern staircases were installed.

In 1962 the Technical College opened on Gravel Hill on the previous site of the National School. The National School's brick and flint building was erected in 1849 by the 'National Society for the Education of the Poor in the Principles of the Established Church', as the school had previously been housed in the Kenton Theatre. The main building of the National School, photographed here by the Director for Education in Oxfordshire in 1904, housed the boys and the infants.

The new building in Gravel Hill was described in 1861 as 'capable of accommodating 520 of both sexes, besides two sets of apartments for the master and mistress'. This was the room used for the infants at the National School.

The girls' rooms at the National School, which now houses the Drama Department of The Henley College. The girls' part of the school, built in 1879, backed onto Gravel Hill and, while the National School occupied the site, it formed the main entrance to the school.

There were gardens stretching between the girls' part of the school, shown above, and the main building. In later years the National School also had gardens in front of the main building, as the grounds used to stretch as far as Deanfield Avenue, then a cinder track. Backing onto the track were flower plots, fruit trees and vegetables, kept tidy by the boys; they were allowed to take any vegetables that they had grown home with them, to help their families. Concealing the gardens from the school were a magnificent row of walnut trees that produced a plentiful crop of nuts. 'We weren't supposed to eat them', remembers Joyce Higgins, a pupil at the National from 1925-1934, 'but of course we all did. The boys used to ask to go to the toilet just before break, so they could get them first.'

The Technical College shared the premises on Gravel Hill with seven classes from the Secondary Modern School from 1960 until February 1961. Builders then gradually began to finish the various Technical College classrooms. Above are third-year craft practice students from 1961, at work inside one of the already finished rooms in the new premises. From left to right, back row: W. Milligan. Middle row: Huhter, F. Cooke. Front row: Wells.

F. Cooke is shown marking out the profile of a gauge at the 1961 Open Day. D. Moore is discussing a precision-fitting exercise with the lecturer, Sam Blundell. Mr Blundell worked at the College for over twenty-five years, beginning his time with the organisation while it was still based in the Reading Road, eventually becoming head of the Department of Engineering and Construction.

Right: Unlocking the doors at the opening of the South Oxfordshire Technical College (SOTC) in 1962. The College had by now fully taken over the old site of the National School, which by then was known as Henley Secondary Modern School. In September 1962 it became possible to offer full-time further education courses for school-leavers and two courses were launched. One was a pre-apprenticeship course for boys of fifteen wanting to enter engineering and the other was a commercial course for boys and girls.

Below: This view of the Technical College shows its main entrance; when the building held the National School this opened out onto Gravel Hill. The steps shown were thus built up to the terrace. Initially, the College address was still Gravel Hill, but a little later the cinder track up the side of the building was turned into Deanfield Avenue and its address then changed.

Technical College students work on a Morris Minor Power Unit as part of an Open Day display in April 1963.

A group of students from 1970, in front of the Technical College minibus. There were 1,600 full- and part-time enrolments at the College that year, with fifteen full-time members of staff. Classes were also being run for the sixth form of the Henley Grammar School, including engineering, drawing, pottery and speedwriting.

The motor vehicle group from the summer of 1971, with their lecturer, John Hocking, seated on the far right. A training course for motor vehicle apprentices had only begun at the College in the previous year and a new workshop was completed by 1970. The workshop marked the last of any major building work at the SOTC and from then on it was a constant struggle to accommodate ever-growing numbers of students within the College.

Above: Keep-fit class in September 1977 under instruction by Dulcie Walsingham, in the centre at the back. After the merger of the SOTC and King James's College, Dulcie Walsingham continued teaching at The Henley College and is currently one of its longest serving members of staff.

Right: Pottery student with her tutor, Kaye McArthur. These classes were held at SOTC Art and Design Centre, which had originally been the Henley Infants School and went on to became the Southfield site of The Henley College. The site was later demolished to make way for a housing estate.

Opposite below: The Technical College had its canteen on the south side of Deanfield Avenue, behind the Youth Centre. The Refectory Block was one of a number of permanent and temporary buildings that sprang up during the 1960s and 1970s, including the Deanfield Block, the Science Laboratory and the Students' Common Room.

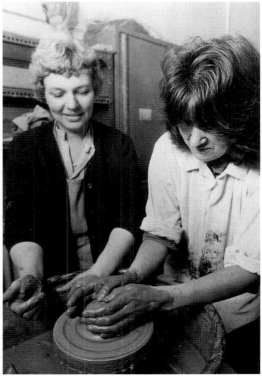

This shot from 1977 shows an art class in progress at the Southfield site of the Technical College. The two men talking to a student by the door on the right of the photograph are, from left to right, Reg Judd, head of Adult Education, and the new College principal, Graham Philips.

Brian Fenwick, head of the Department of Business Studies and General Education at the SOTC, with a group of secretarial students in 1977. The College organisation had been divided into two departments back in 1970, the other being the Department of Engineering and Building, later known as Engineering and Construction.

A secretarial class at the South Oxfordshire Technical College, with their tutor Joyce Ramsey seen at the back in the centre.

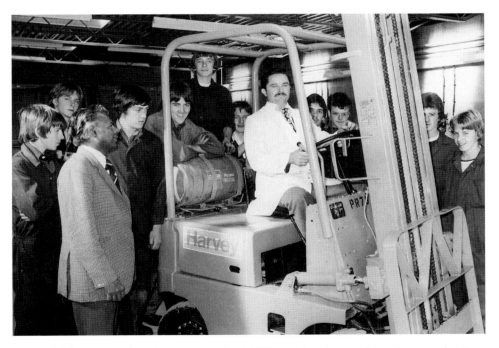

The fork-lift truck engineering course at the SOTC was hugely popular and here a class is seen with their engineering tutors. John Sutton is seated at the control of the truck, while Parkie Da Silva can be seen on the left of the photograph.

The integrated training course for fork-lift truck mechanics was not available at any other College in the country and the *Reading Mercury* recorded that in 1977 two students 'this term have made the journey respectively from St Austell, Cornwall and Manchester'.

The SOTC building seen before the merger of 1987, when a variety of new premises were erected. Graham Philips, last principal of the Technical College, was chosen to become principal of the new Henley College. At the end of the Technical College's existence Graham Philips said how excited he was to be combining the best of two traditions to create a new college, not just in the 'grammar school tradition', but also the 'vocational, applied tradition' of the South Oxfordshire Technical College.

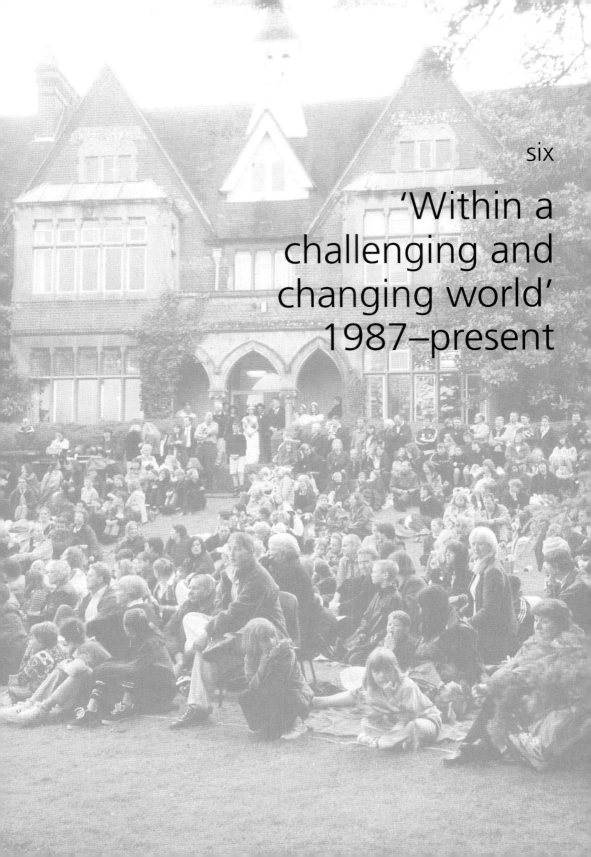

six

'Within a challenging and changing world' 1987–present

The Henley College

September 1987 saw the official opening of The Henley College, following the amalgamation of King James's College and the South Oxfordshire Technical College. The move had its precedent back in the eighteenth century; the Free Grammar School and Dame Periam's Charity School, the College's predecessors, were united in 1778. The aim in 1987 was, as over 200 years before, to create a place of education that would be more responsive to the needs of pupils, parents and employers within Henley-on-Thames and beyond. The original mission statement of The Henley College argued that the new institution was a necessary development 'Within a challenging and changing world'. Many staff from King James's and the Technical College stayed on to work in The Henley College, but there were also numerous developments within the new College; a different academic structure was created for the new institution, with the curriculum divided into five schools of study. The College initially opened its doors in 1987 to about 1,500 full-time students. Today the numbers of students are still growing, alongside an ever-developing range of courses spread over the two different sites of The Henley College.

The centrepiece of the new college was the £1.2 million new building, sitting alongside the old SOTC buildings on Deanfield Avenue. The new building was built on the site of the former Technical College car park and its facilities included an Art and Design centre and a social centre for staff and students. This building, together with the old SOTC site, was newly named as the 'Deanfield' site of The Henley College. The former King James's site was now known as 'Rotherfield'.

Right: Graham Philips became the first principal of The Henley College in 1987. 'I feel enormously privileged', he said at the time, 'to be at the start of what I hope will be a very successful new college. Our aim will be to set ourselves the highest possible standard of academic and vocational achievement. I'm confident that we have the staff and students to do so.'

Below: The former SOTC sites on Greys Road were renamed as the 'Southfield' site of the new College. The old chapel, below, had also once been a music hall, and from 1987 it housed the College's media and photography courses. The Southfield site was sold by the College in 1998 to make way for low-cost housing.

Above: The catering training kitchen at the Southfield site. The kitchen and restaurant were moved in 1998 to the new Deanfield site and renamed *Blades* Restaurant.

Right: John Holtorp as Prospero and Lisa Jayne-Jones as Ariel from *The Tempest*, a production which formed part of the College's second European drama tour of 1988. The College's theatre company undertook an ambitious tour of Germany, Austria, Czechoslovakia and Hungary, performing in a variety of venues from the garden of the British Embassy in Prague, professional theatres in Salzburg, Prague and Brno as well as a hilltop temple in Budapest. The programme consisted of two Shakespeare productions, *A Midsummer Night's Dream* and *The Tempest*, directed by Steve Keating and Peter Allen respectively, with two casts, musicians and crew.

Above: The Snow-Go Project of 1990 was run by the College's health studies students. Together with Shirley Stevens, the BTEC group raised thousands of pounds to take seven special-needs students skiing in Kaprun. The seven, from the College's special-needs department, had never been abroad with their peer group before and spent an unforgettable week skiing, swimming, ice-skating and bowling in Austria.

Left: Debbie Crossfield, leaning from the left, and Helene Whitehall in a scene from *Speak No Evil*, which was performed at the Olivier Theatre in the National in 1990 as part of the Lloyds Bank Theatre Challenge. The play was devised by the whole group and directed by fellow student Vicky Udall.

The College choir and orchestra toured Austria in 1991 and sang the Haydn Mass in St Peter's Church, Salzburg. Alex Taylor, a College student, played the grand organ once played by Mozart. Alex was a finalist in the Young Musician of the Year competition and went on to give recitals in Wigmore Hall and The Purcell Room, as well as broadcasting on Classic FM and Radio 3.

Archbishop Trevor Huddleston gave an impassioned Henley College Lecture in St Mary's Church in 1992 on apartheid in South Africa. He is seen here chatting afterwards to College students.

The first European Youth Conference Organising Committee in 1992. For the next five years, students at the College organised Youth Conferences and invited fellow student delegates from all over Europe to attend a week-long conference hosted by the College.

A large group of College students visited Seville in Spain for Expo '92. The students were invited to attend the event and not only saw all the international exhibits but also participated in a Youth Parliament.

The first group of successful International Baccalaureate students receiving their certificates in 1992. The course was launched at the College in 1990 and the IB quickly became popular with both local and international students.

Above: The Henley College synchronised swimming team who won the English Schools Swimming Championships in 1994.

Right: As part of the Henley College Lecture series in 1995, the broadcaster and *Newsnight* presenter Jeremy Paxman gave a talk to a packed Rotherfield Hall on the media. Paxman was faced with searching questions from students on his unique interviewing style but was, naturally, unphased by any exchanges.

Opposite below: The Henley College encourages work experience in other countries. Students from the BTEC National Art and Design course visited Italy and are photographed at the Italia Cattalan studios in Vicenza. Their lecturer, Phil Bird, is seated on the right.

College students on an Austrian exchange, photographed in 1995 on the slopes of the Schmittenhohe in Zell-am-See. This exchange programme was started in 1993 by Gerlinde Tomazej of the Handelsakademie in Zell and Shirley Stevens and Peter Allen of the College and has offered a unique opportunity for College students to ski with their Austrian hosts.

David Ferraro together with his wife Alison, to the left, and colleague Olga Sheen on a classical studies trip. He organised these trips for enthusiastic students who enjoyed his scholarly guide to the classical antiquities and sites. Dave sadly died in 1996, closely followed by his wife a few weeks later. As a great teacher, scholar and friend he was mourned by countless students who appreciated his encouragement, support and deep interest in their future success. 'Mr Ferraro provided me with all the support I could ask for and more', commented one student, 'Where would my Aeneas have settled without his Anchises?'

Terri Chilton, Foundation Art and Design student, won the Orga Card competition in 1996 to produce a winning design for a Smart telephone card. Terri is pictured here, right of centre, with representatives from the company. Terri's design, called *Blades and Flags*, was reproduced as limited edition prints. Prints have been presented as gifts to visiting speakers and also hang in many of the College's partner institutions across Europe.

Sir Ron Dearing visited the College in 1996 to give his views on A Level reform. Dearing had the job of chairing a Government committee on the subject and he was able to express his views to students prior to the publication of The Dearing Report. From left to right, back row: Katherine Statham, Aaron Mannion. Front row: Caroline Montford, Emma Godfrey.

Matthew Pinsent, Olympic Gold medalist, contributed to a sports forum on the theme of 'Olympians Past, Present and Future' for the 1996 European Youth Conference. He shared a platform with fellow gold medallist Steve Redgrave and their coach Jurgen Grobler together with Olympic skiers Ronald Duncan and Graham Bell.

Henley College students Ben Causer and Stuart Cripps won the Badminton National Championships in 1997, winning the gold medal after dropping only one game. The College also subsequently won the gold medal in this event in 1998 and 1999.

Lord Yehudi Menuhin gave the Dame Periam Lecture in 1997. The lecture, in honour of the College's seventeenth-century founder, is an annual part of a series of lectures held at the College. Lord Menuhin was photographed on the terrace at Rotherfield with the College's director of music, Christopher Walker, on the left and the principal, Graham Phillips, on the right.

A Geography field trip to Sweden for A Level and International Baccaluareate students in 1997, which involved the study of forest ecology and glaciation features.

Right: The world-renowned cybernetics expert, Professor Kevin Warwick of Reading University, gave an enthralling Henley College Lecture in 1997, demonstrating his intelligent robots to students. Professor Warwick, on the left, is pictured with the College principal, Graham Phillips, on the right.

Below: Students receiving their awards for the European Youth Initiative at the Wycombe Swan Theatre in 1997 from television presenter Jenny Hull. The project had involved working with other students in Germany, Austria and Italy to research and produce a leisure guide for young people. The Henley College students had travelled through eight countries in the course of the project, luckily finding time to ski in Austria. On their return to Henley they produced a guide in several languages entitled *Go Eurown Way*, with an accompanying professionally-made video.

Above: Students helping to demolish the old engineering block on the Deanfield site. They were filmed by Central TV and featured on their evening news, as the ground was prepared for the new £4.8 million building on this site.

Left: The new buildings at Deanfield opened in 1998. They housed a new College restaurant, *Blades* Restaurant, as well as an IT centre and a variety of classrooms.

One of the annual musicals performed every year at the College in December, *Grease* played to packed houses in Rotherfield Hall in 1998. About 100 students were involved in this memorable show, which had the audience literally dancing in the aisles.

Skiing is a popular sport at the College and its ski team annually competes at the British Schoolgirls' Championships in Flaine, France. The two teams for the 2001 races were, from left to right: Emily Howard, Maya Herbolzheimer, Cate Poulson, Caroline Chilton, Daisy Venn and Amy Curl.

College students run their own radio station, HOT AIR FM, which broadcasts to Henley and surrounding areas. This has run for four years since 2000 and gives many students the opportunity to learn live broadcasting techniques. Boris Johnson, editor of *The Spectator* and MP for Henley-on-Thames, was one of the guests to be invited into the studio in 2001 to give a live interview.

Students from The Henley College always attend the annual Oxfordshire Sixth Form Conference. The 2001 Conference was held at University College, Oxford.

December 2001 saw a College production of Stephen Sondheim's *Sweeney Todd – The Demon Barber of Fleet Street* start a week-long run at the local Kenton Theatre. This was the first time a production from The Henley College had been performed in the local theatre, continuing a traditional association with the Kenton that had been shared by its predecessors, Henley Grammar School and King James's College.

A scene from the College's 2001 production of the Greek tragedy, *Antigone*. Directed by Nic Saunders, performances were inititially staged at local venues such as Fawley Court and Braziers Park, before the students left for Tolo in Greece. The island, just off the Greek mainland, provided a stunning background for the production, which proved an unforgettable experience for all involved.

The victorious College rugby team in 2001, who comfortably beat Magdalen College School in the Oxfordshire Cup final, pictured here with their coach Danny Batty. The College's rugby squad are part of the Sports Development Programme which was launched at the College in 2001. The Programme initially included three sports, rugby, rowing and skiing, and later was extended to include football and tennis. It allows participating students extra hours of coaching, fitness training and motivational sessions each week, on top of their academic timetable, to develop their sporting abilities.

David Ansell became the new principal of The Henley College in 2001. He had been one of the team of inspectors that had visited the College in 1997 and so already knew the special and unique character of the College.

The Golden Jubilee in May 2002 was marked by a production on the lawn at Rotherfield, involving College students as well as 200 local primary schoolchildren. The show was written by Alfie Hay and students from The Henley College sang and danced in the lead roles.

Above: The victorious four in the quad sculls in the National Schools Regatta in 2003 at Holme Pierrepoint, Nottingham. Apart from being students at the College and on the Sports Development Programme, they also row for Henley's Leander Rowing Club. From left to right: J. Halsall, N. Clark, T. Wilkinson, R. Davis.

Left: Within The Henley College there still hangs a copy of the Royal Charter of James I, which marked the foundation of the Free Grammar School of Henley-on-Thames in 1604. The present Henley College in many ways shares the same educational standards as the Free Grammar School, for the Charter states that the Henley school should provide 'good learning to endure for ever in time to come'.

Other local titles published by Tempus

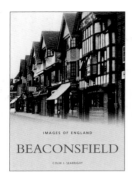

Beaconsfield
COLIN J. SEABRIGHT

Using over 200 archive images, this detailed volume illustrates just how much Beaconsfield has changed over the last century. The selection includes vistas of well-known streets like London Road, Warwick Road, Ledborough Lane and Penn Road, alongside postcard views of shops, places of worship, public houses and historic inns. Sporting activities, royal visits and local people are also recorded.

7524 3093 9

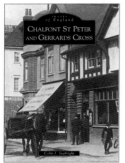

Chalfont St Peter and Gerrards Cross
COLIN J. SEABRIGHT

Illustrated with over 200 photographs and postcards, this fascinating collection captures the twentieth-century history of the two adjacent villages of Chalfont St Peter and Gerrards Cross – from the shops and businesses that evolved from the market village of Chalfont St Peter to the rapid growth and development of Gerrards Cross into a thriving commuter village, which came with the opening of the railway in 1906.

7524 2493 9

Oxford United Football Club
JON MURRAY

Oxford United is a club with a remarkable history. This book contains over 220 images that illustrate the fascinating football heritage that belongs to Oxford United – from the early days of Headington United until the modern-day side on the verge of departure from its traditional home. This book shows many of the great moments in the club's history, and is essential reading for anyone with a long-standing acquaintance with the club.

7524 1183 7

Royal Grammar School, High Wycombe
J.I. MITCHELL

The Royal Grammar School, High Wycombe, will celebrate the 450th anniversary of its royal charter in 2012. Though pictures of the original hospital of St John have not survived, this book provides a pictorial history of its successor, the town's grammar school, from the mid-nineteenth century to present day. This collection of photographs will be of interest to pupils, staff and anyone with an affection for High Wycombe and its story.

7524 2861 6

If you are interested in purchasing other books published by Tempus, or in case you have difficulty finding any Tempus books in your local bookshop, you can also place orders directly through our website

www.tempus-publishing.com

or from   **BOOKPOST**, Freepost, PO Box 29, Douglas, Isle of Man, IM99 1BQ
tel 01624 836000   email bookshop@enterprise.net